EASY
PIANO

WALT DISNEY PICTURES AND WA...
present
THE CHRONICLE...

NARNIA

THE LION, THE WITCH AND THE WARDROBE

MUSIC COMPOSED BY HARRY GREGSON-WILLIAMS

ISBN-13: 978-1-4234-2774-2
ISBN-10: 1-4234-2774-2

WONDERLAND MUSIC COMPANY, INC.

7777 W. BLUEMOUND RD. P.O. BOX 13819 MILWAUKEE, WI 53213

Visit Hal Leonard Online at
www.halleonard.com

THE LION, THE WITCH AND THE WARDROBE

EVACUATING LONDON

Music by HARRY GREGSON-WILLIAMS

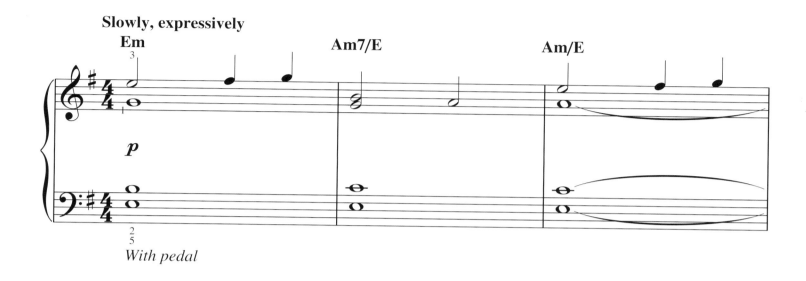

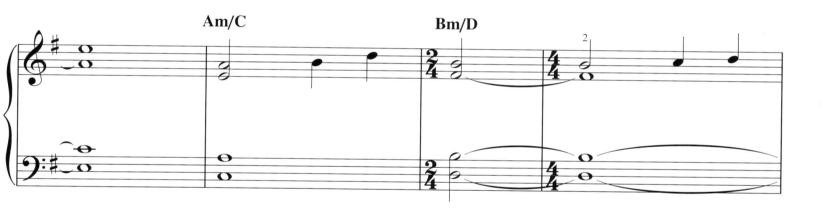

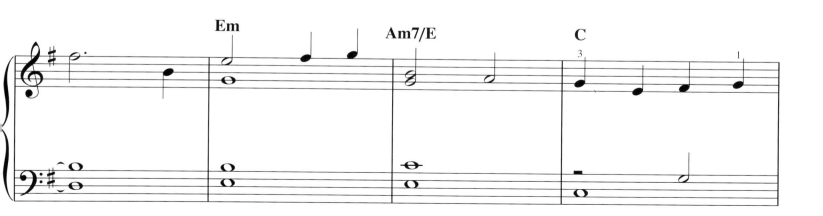

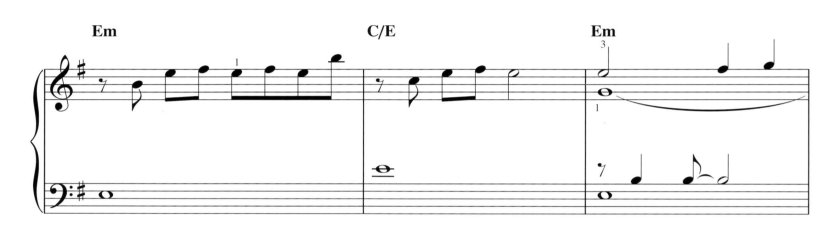

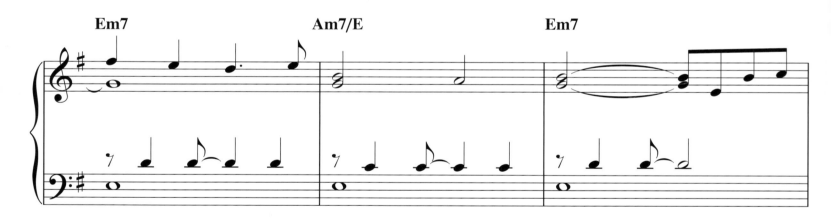

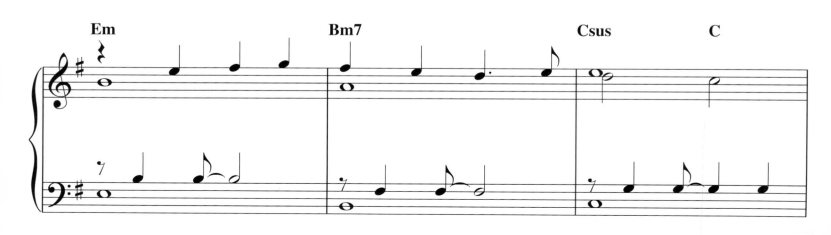

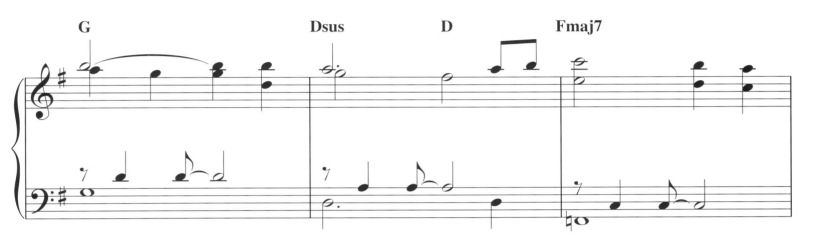

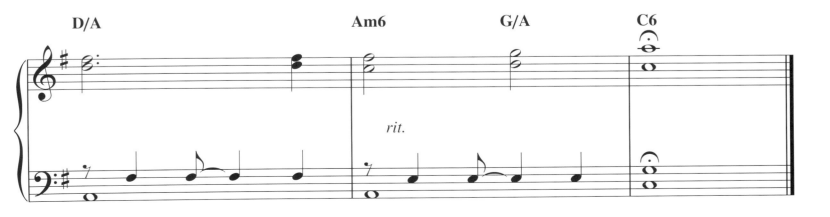

A NARNIA LULLABY

Music by HARRY GREGSON-WILLIAMS

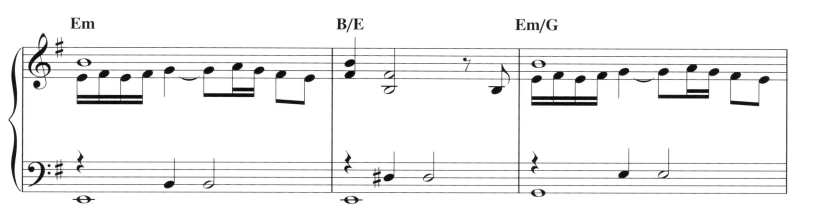

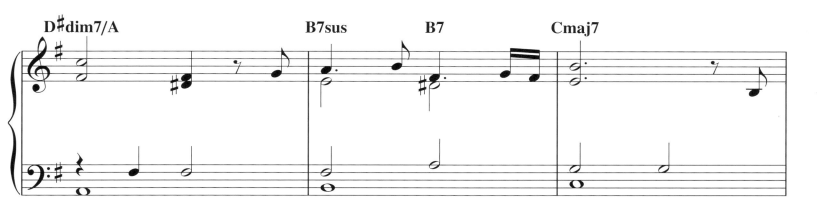

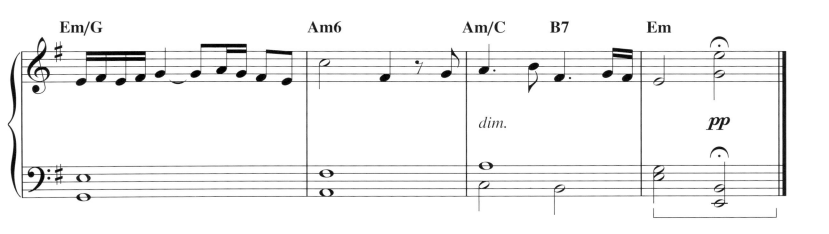

LUCY MEETS MR. TUMNUS

Music by HARRY GREGSON-WILLIAMS

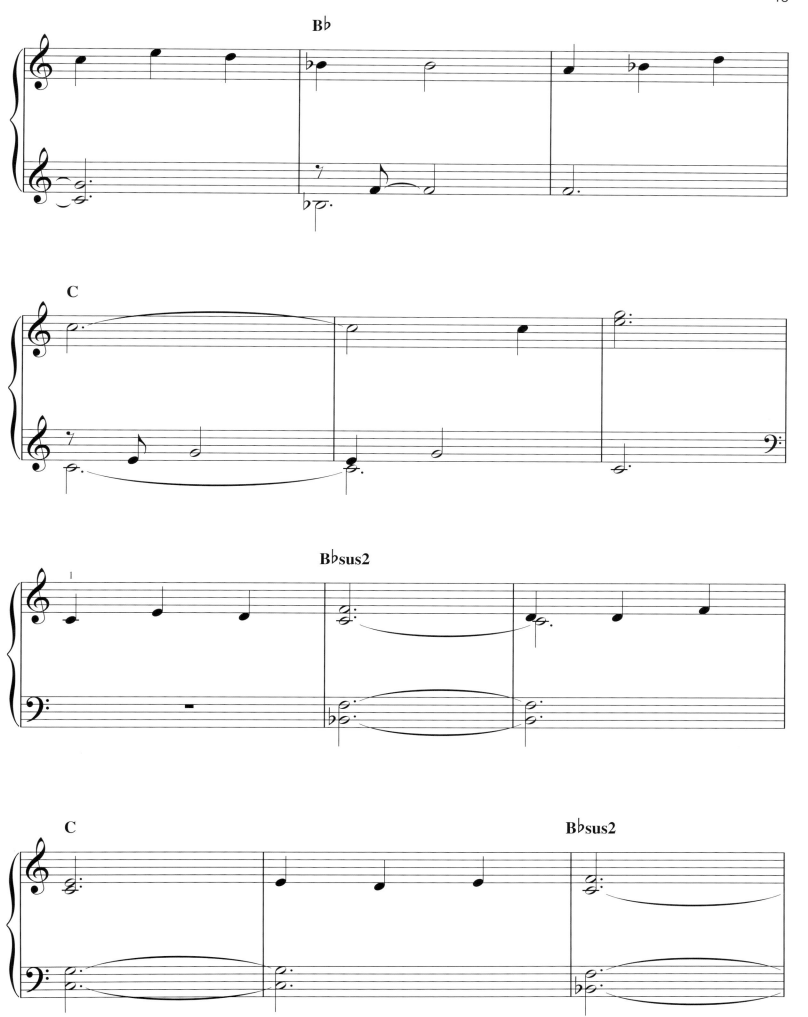

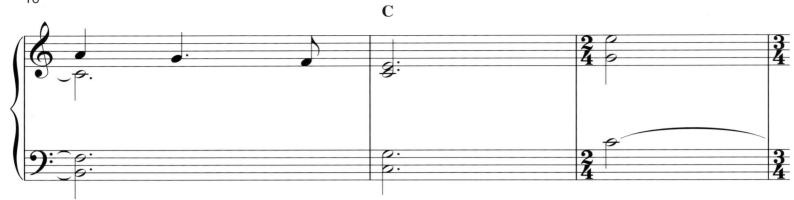

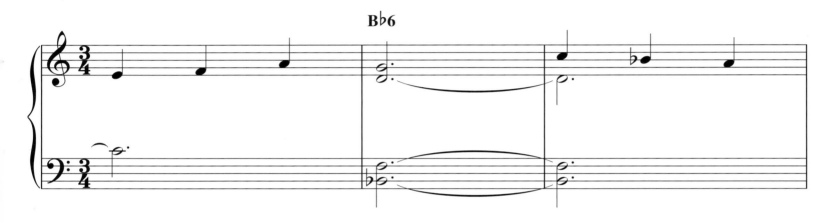

WUNDERKIND

Words and Music by
ALANIS MORISSETTE

first to take this foot to vir - gin snow.____
best back pock - et's se - cret, our bond, full - blown.__
view a - bout - face, wheth - er great will be__ done.__

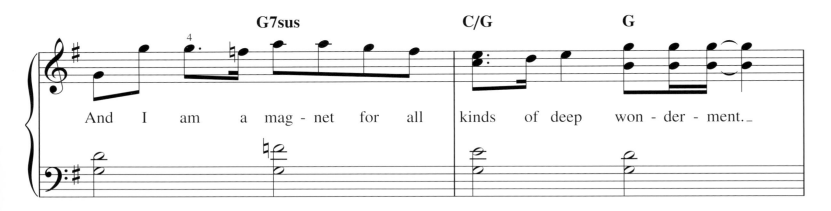

And I am a mag - net for all kinds of deep won - der - ment.__

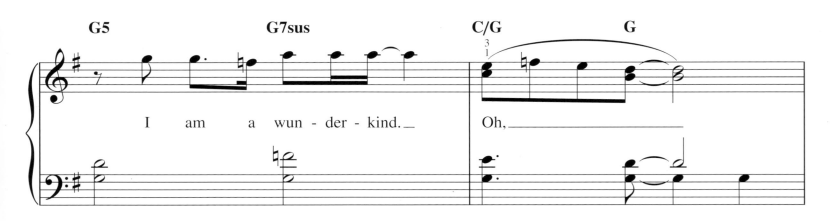

I am a wun - der - kind.__ Oh,____

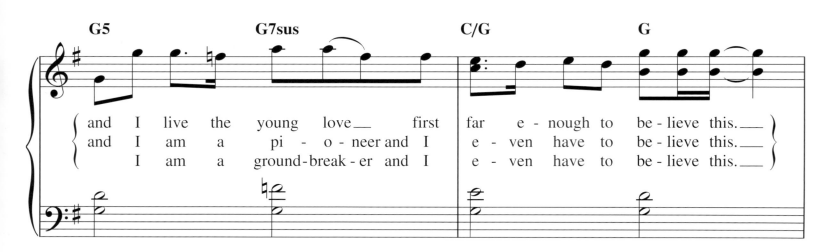

and I live the young love__ first far e - nough to be - lieve this.__
and I am a pi - o - neer and I e - ven have to be - lieve this.__
I am a ground - break - er and I e - ven have to be - lieve this.__

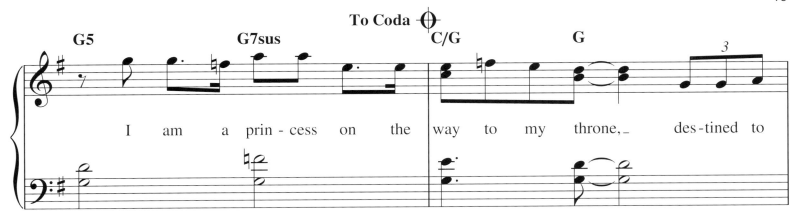

D.S. al Coda

Most beau - ti - ful

way to my throne. ___ And I am a mag - net for all

kinds of deep won - der - ment. ___ I am a wun - der - kind. ___

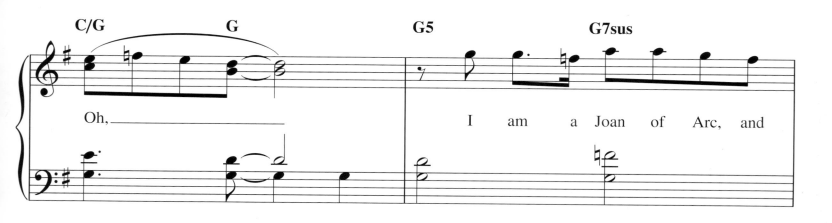

Oh, _____ I am a Joan of Arc, and

smart e-nough to be-lieve this.___ I am a prin-cess on the

way to my throne,___ des-tined to reign, des-tined to

roam. Des-tined to reign,

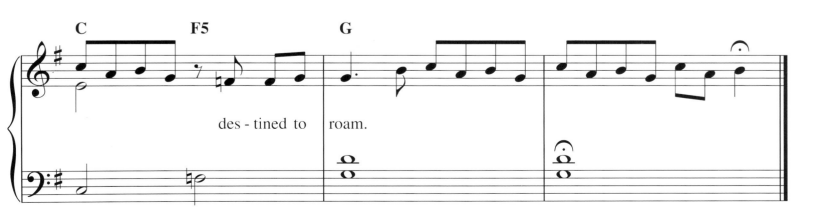

des-tined to roam.

FATHER CHRISTMAS

Music by HARRY GREGSON-WILLIAMS

Moderately fast

With pedal

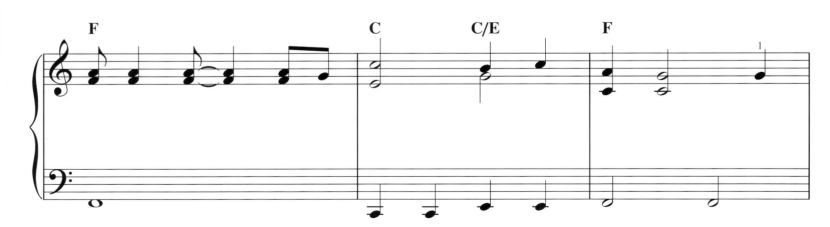

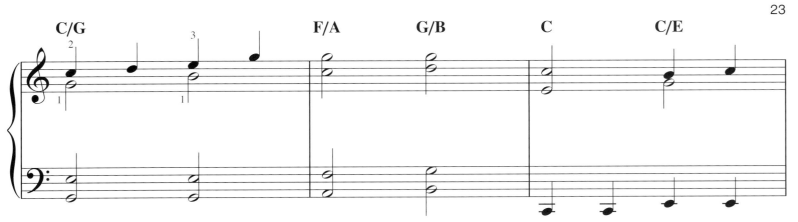

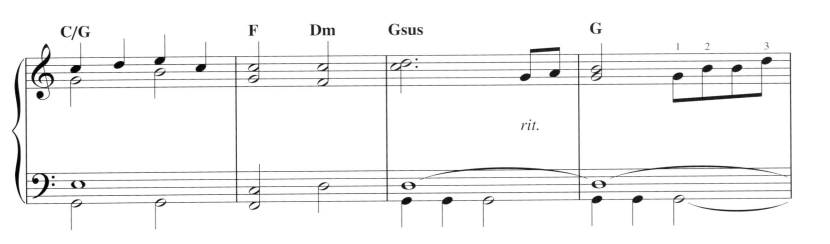

Moderately slow, more expressively

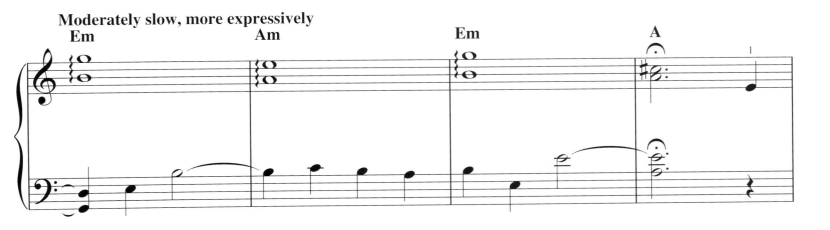

24

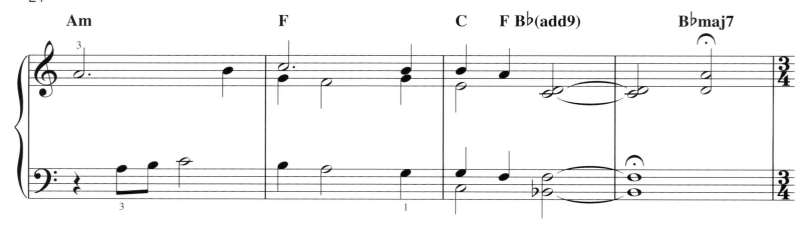

Moderately slow

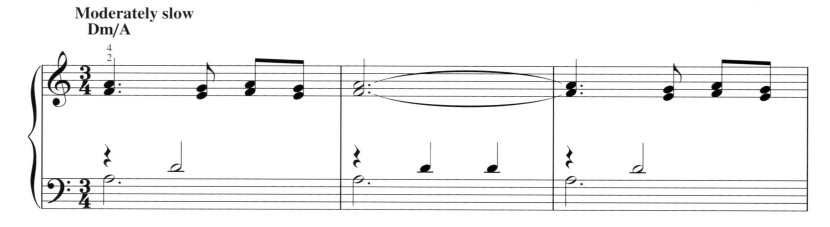

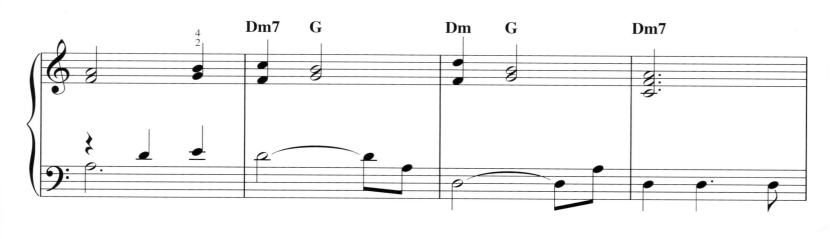

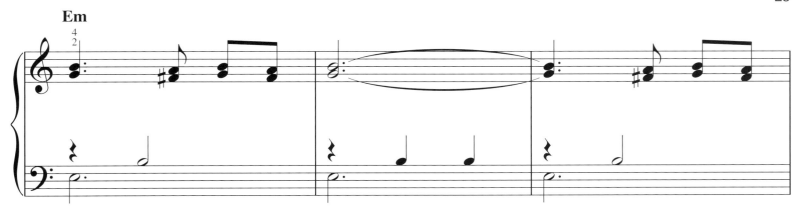

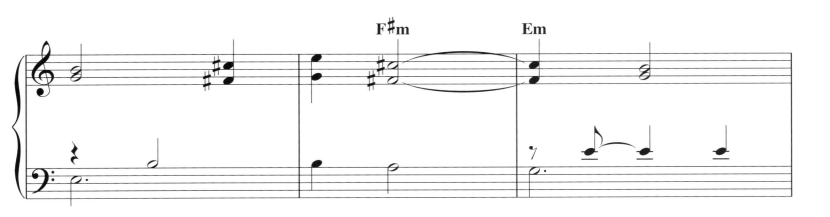

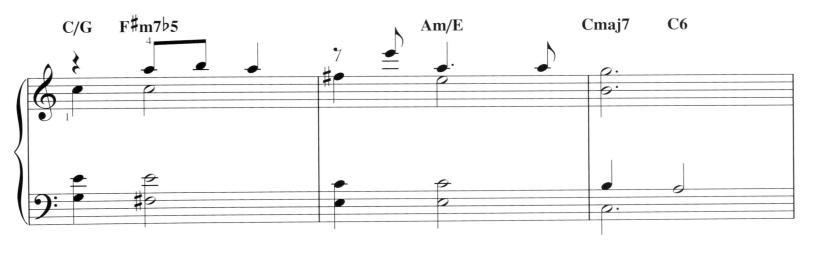

CAN'T TAKE IT IN

Written by IMOGEN HEAP
and HARRY GREGSON-WILLIAMS

Moderately, in 2

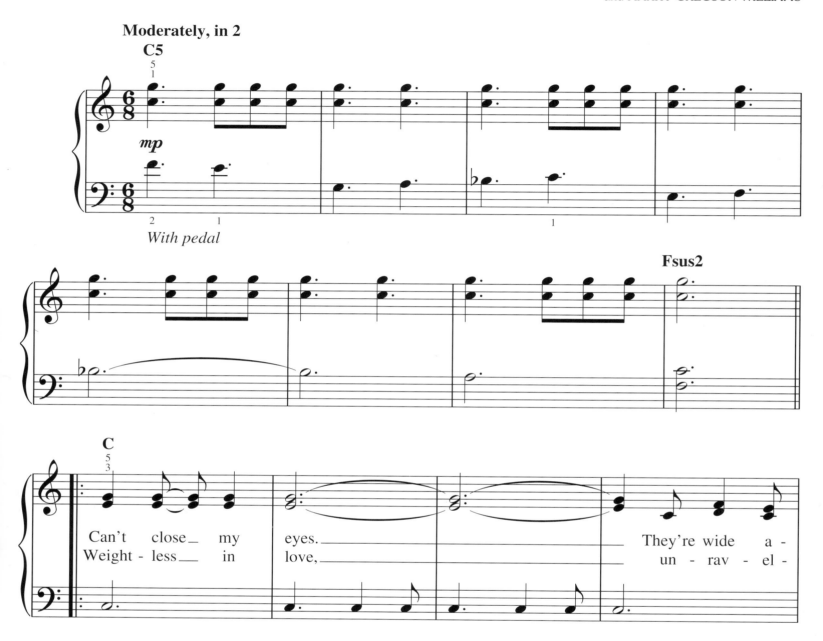

With pedal

Lyrics:
Can't close my eyes. They're wide a-wake.
Weight-less in love, un-rav-el-ing, Ev-'ry for

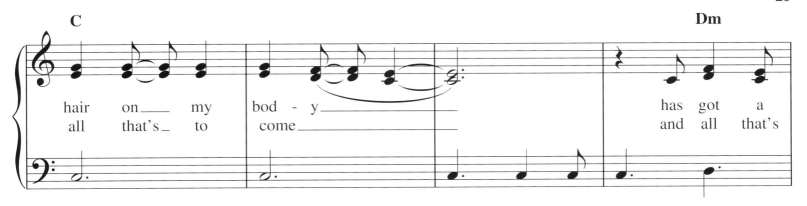

hair on____ my bod - y_____ has got a
all that's_ to come_____ and all that's

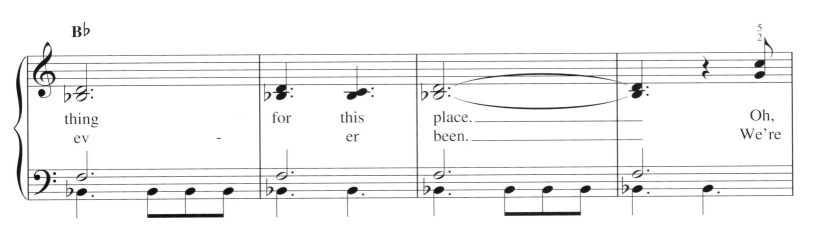

thing for this place._____ Oh,
ev - er been._____ We're

emp - ty____ my heart; I've got to____ make
back to___ the board, with ev - er - y

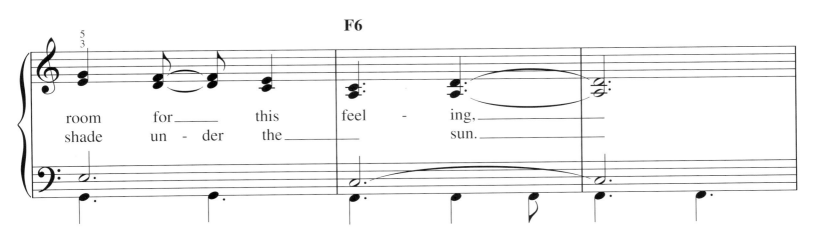

room for____ this feel - ing,_____
shade un - der the____ sun._____

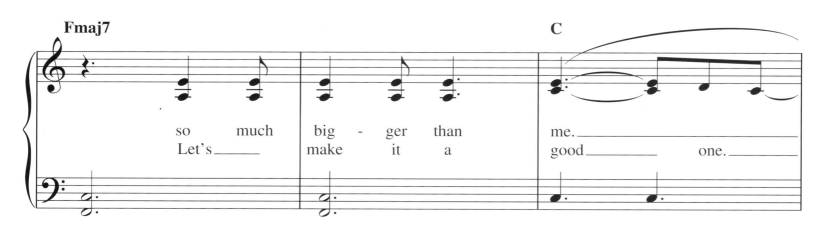

so much   big - ger than   me.____

Let's____ make   it   a   good____   one.____

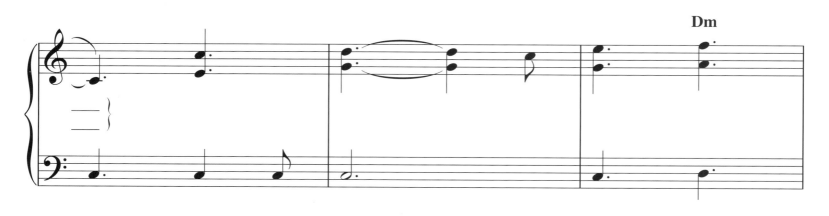

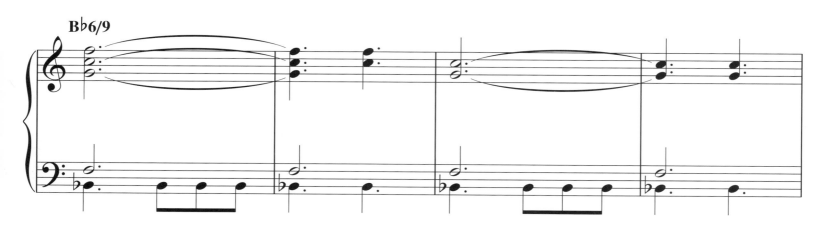

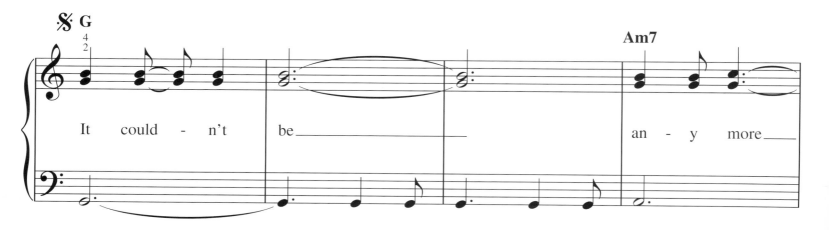

It   could - n't   be_____   an - y   more____

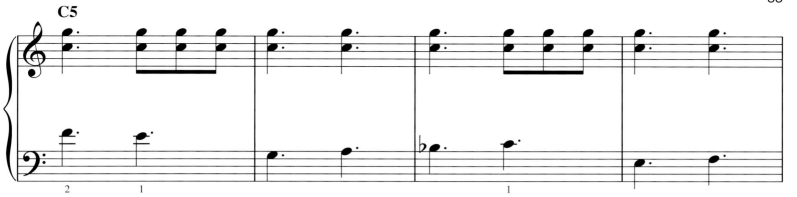

D.S. al Coda
(take 2nd ending)

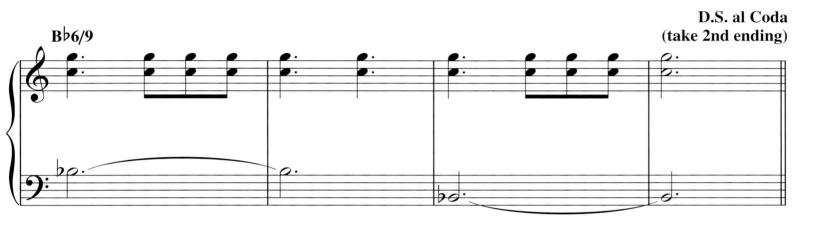

WHERE

Music and Lyrics by HARRY GREGSON-WILLIAMS
and LISBETH SCOTT

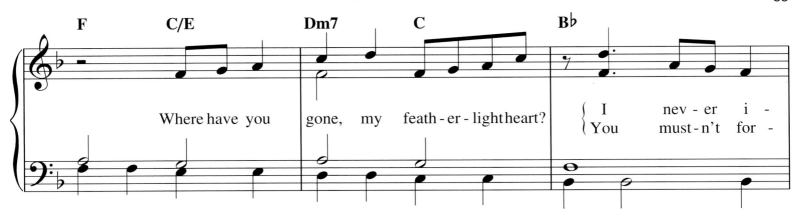

Where have you gone, my feath-er-light heart?

{ I nev-er i-
{ You must-n't for-

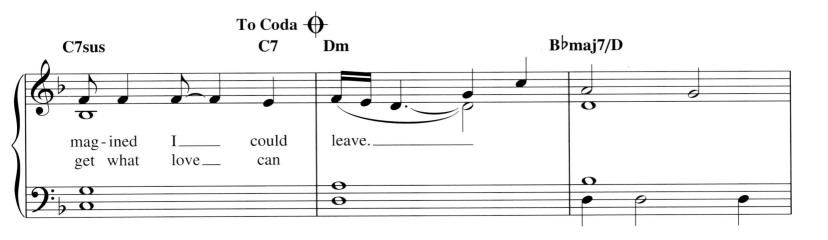

mag-ined I____ could
get what love____ can

leave.____

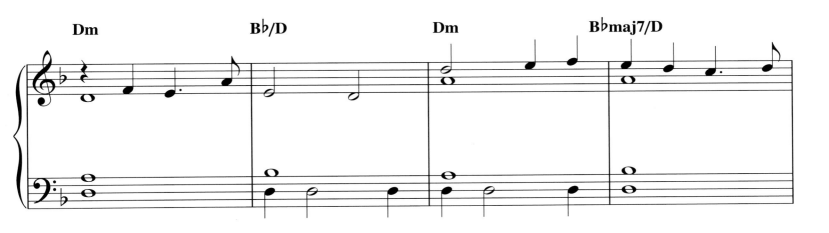

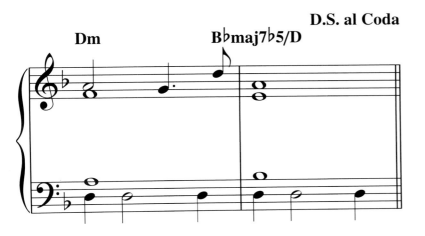

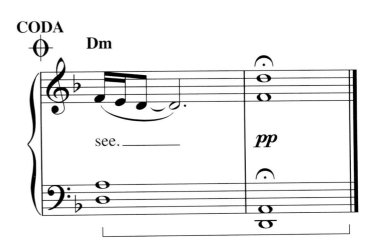

see.____

pp

WINTER LIGHT

Words and Music by
TIM FINN

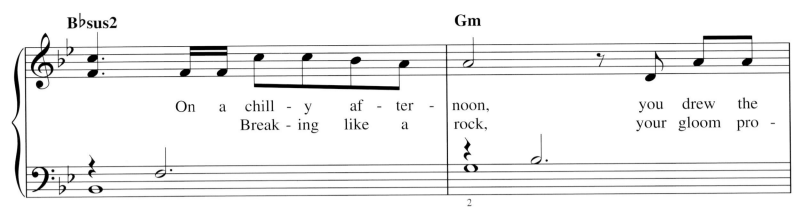

B♭sus2　　　　　　　　　　　　　**Gm**

On a chill - y af - ter - noon,　　　you drew the
Break - ing like a rock,　　　your gloom pro -

F　　　　　　　　　　　　　　　　　　**C**　　　**Am**

blind.
found.　　　　The earth was fro - zen,

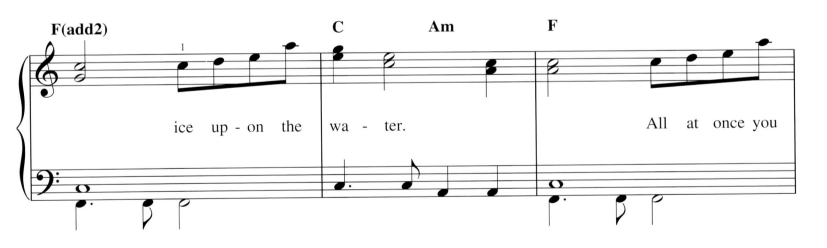

F(add2)　　　　　**C**　　　**Am**　　　**F**

ice up - on the wa - ter.　　　All at once you

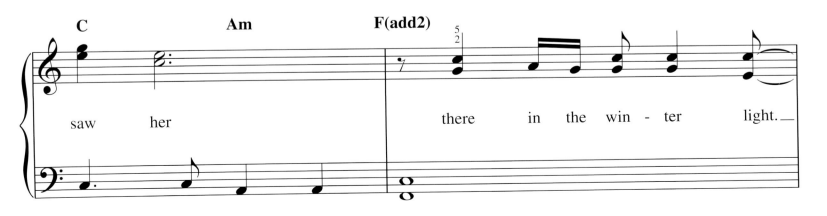

C　　　**Am**　　　**F(add2)**

saw her　　　there in the win - ter light.

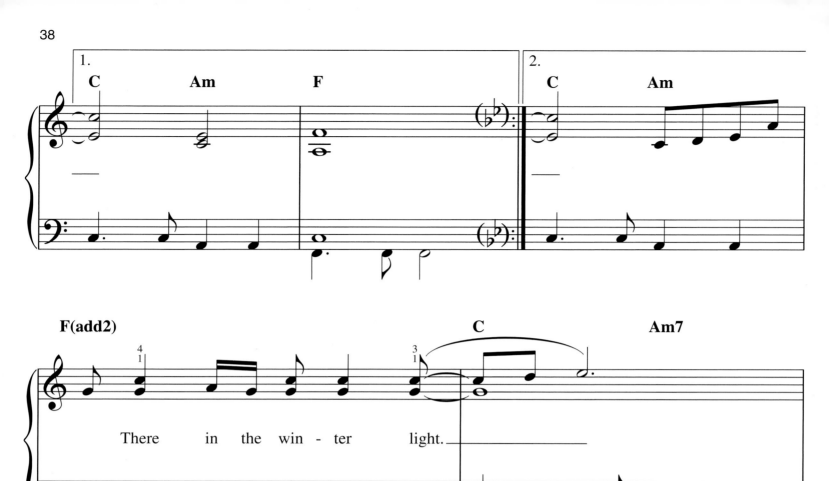

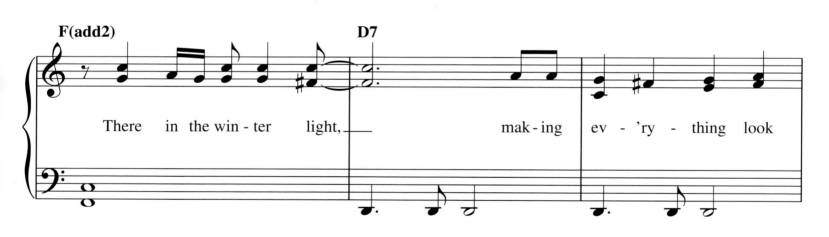

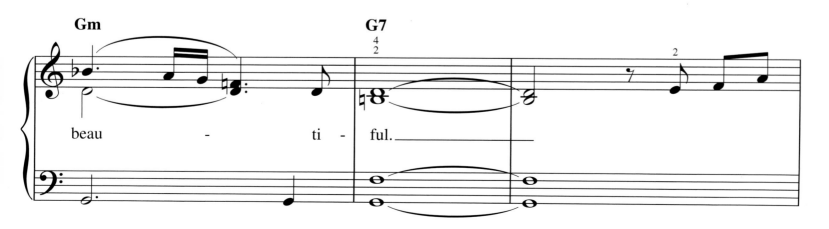

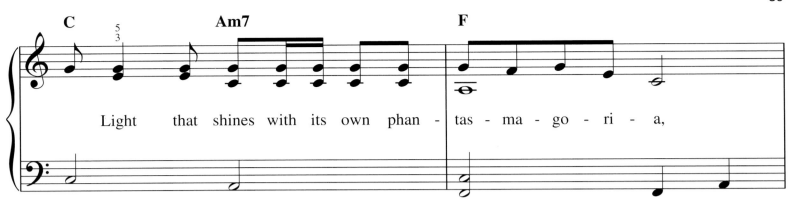

Light that shines with its own phan - tas - ma - go - ri - a,

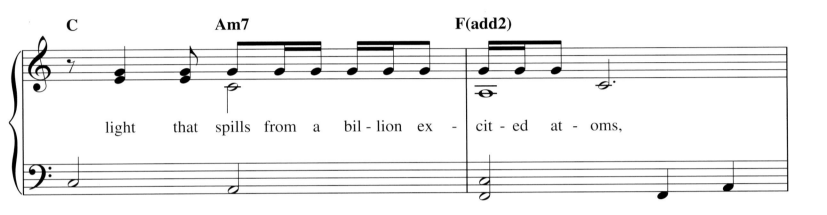

light that spills from a bil - lion ex - cit - ed at - oms,

light that lin - gers in a qui - et room, re - veal for me; shine

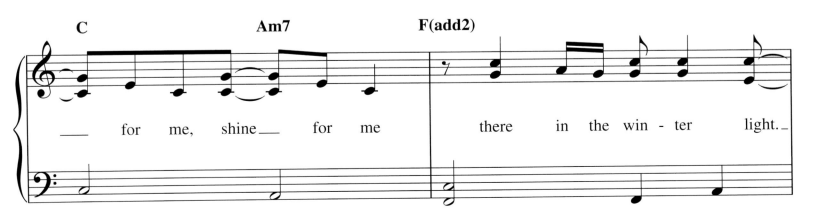

for me, shine for me there in the win - ter light.

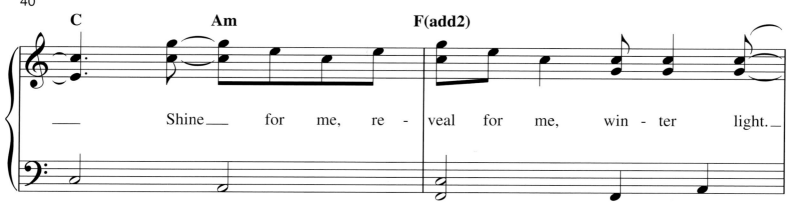

Shine___ for me, re - veal for me, win - ter light.___

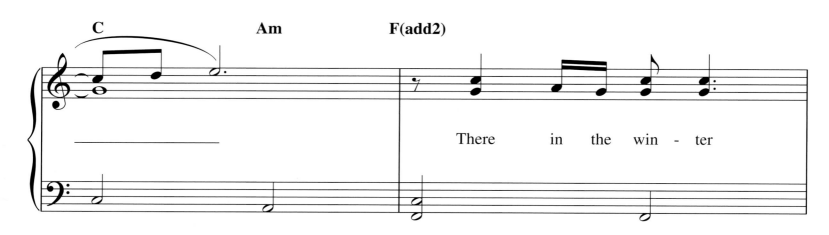

_____ There in the win - ter

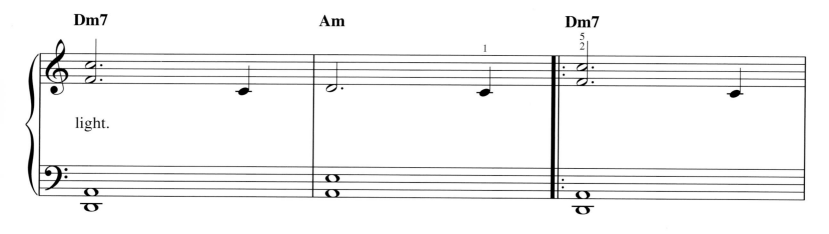

light.

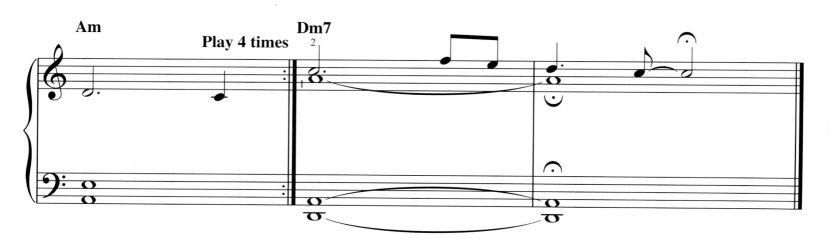

Play 4 times